SOOTHING SOAPS

SOOTHING
SOAPS

FOR HEALTHY SKIN

SANDY MAINE

Soothing Soaps for Healthy Skin
by Sandy Maine

Photo props courtesy of EsScentuals of Fort Collins, CO

Cover design: Elizabeth Mrofka
Photography: Joe Coca
Production: Dean Howes

 Interweave Press, Inc.
201 East Fourth Street
Loveland, Colorado, 80537-5655
USA

Printed in Hong Kong by Sing Cheong

Library of Congress Cataloging-in-Publication Data
    Maine, Sandy
        Soothing soaps for healthy skin/Sandy Maine
           p.   cm.
        Includes bibliographical references (p. 93) and index.
        ISBN 1-883010-36-5 (pbk.)
        1. Soap.   I. Title.
TP991.M265   1997
668'. 124—dc21   97–36761
                                                  CIP

First Printing: 10M:1097:CC

With gratitude and appreciation for beauty,

in its every expression, and to all hourglasses emptied of sand.

INTRODUCTION

Soapmaking is an almost magical endeavor that transforms oils, fats, and other ingredients into pure, fragrant, useful bars. As you try your hand at creating these healing recipes, you will see the disparate materials blend and enrich each other, forming soaps that are soothing, clean, and peaceful. As you mix in your own thoughts, love, and sensibilities, you will find that you've created a soap unlike any other. Along the way, you will receive generous effective healing gifts that you, in turn, can pass on to others.

Seventeen years ago I made my first batch of soap on our kitchen table. I was astonished to see real soap—even though it wasn't excellent soap—arise from such unlovely ingredients: oil and household lye. Fascinated, I learned everything I could about soap: its history, lore, and chemistry, and the many ways to use it. I experimented with many soapmaking recipes, methods, and variations. Eventually my soapmaking became a business, SunFeather Soaps, with three buildings and a staff of fifteen. I feel that I myself have been transformed, in a wonderful, adventuresome way I could not have anticipated, and now I hope the same may come about for you.

TABLE OF CONTENTS

Chapter One: The Healing Nature of Homemade Soap   13

Chapter Two: Loving Your Skin   19

Chapter Three: Flower Power: Healing Gifts from the Garden   25

Chapter Four: Naturally Healing Soaps   35

Antiseptic Soaps   39

*Common Plantain Soap • Goldenseal Soap • Cloud's Healing Soap
White Cedar Soap • Tea Tree Antiseptic Soap*

Poison Ivy Soaps   47

*Calamine Soap • Jewelweed Soap • Camphor and Clary Sage Soap
Balsam of Peru and Benzoin Anti-Itch Soap • Witch Hazel Soap*

Soaps for Blemished Skin   55

*Lavender and Rosemary Soap • Chamomile, Sage, and Laminaria Seaweed Scrub Cleanser
Juniper Soap • Self-Heal Soap • Ylang-Ylang and Frankincense Soap*

Soothing Emollient Healing Soaps   63

*Baby's Bottom Repair Soap • Fresh Aloe and Nettle Leaf Soap
Oat and Barley Soap • Shea Butter Soap • Pine Tar Soap and Shampoo Bar*

Chapter Five: The Esoterics   71

*Flower Essence Soap • Moonbeam Soap • Lightning Water Soap
Sunflower Soap*

Chapter Six: The Haven of Water   85

Recommended Reading   93

Retail Mail-Order Sources   94

Materials Index   95

Index   96

1

THE HEALING NATURE OF HANDMADE SOAP

One of the uses of soap, I've discovered, is to heal. By decreasing the surface tension of water, soap draws infectious agents, along with other unwanted or irritating substances, away from the skin. When we add healing herbs to soap, we increase its powers to cleanse, soothe, and protect in a natural, healthful way.

Some of my favorite healing soap formulas begin with a clear glycerin base of soponified vegetable oils. It is especially kind to troubled skin. It's also friendly to the soothing herbs, wonderful essences, and special ingredients that I incorporate into the soap. These qualities, plus outstanding ease of use, make glycerin soap base the foundation of each recipe.

For the most part, I'd like you to focus on the healing herbs, the soothing essences, and the simple beauty of the soaps you make. Conse-

This gentle soap is kind to troubled skin and friendly to soothing herbs.

quently, I recommend that you purchase a good glycerin soap base by mail from one of the several sources at the end of this book, or purchase pure, unscented glycerin soap from a natural-products store. These products already incorporate the essential ingredients of soap and require only the addition of herbs and fragrances to become luxuriously complete. For those who wish to make the base themselves, books containing formulas, ingredients, and procedures are listed in the Resource Directory.

The glycerin base is colorless, translucent, and solid; start by melting it gently in a double boiler, over medium heat. Add soothing botanicals, fragrant oils, and any other ingredients that please you, and stir. Then pour the thick liquid into a mold and let it cool.

From the mold comes soap that is lovely to see— translucent, almost glowing, speckled or spotted or striped with its healing herbs. The base is nearly impossible to ruin, and it's affordable. And best of all, there's very little waiting: Your soap creations will be complete and ready to use within an hour!

The exploration of the herbal world is a journey that is both objective and intuitive. Considering that the term "herb" encompasses plants that are used for cooking, fragrance, or healing, the range is enormous. Narrowing the focus to medicinal herbs still gives us plenty of territory, for herbs are the primary source of medicine for most of the world today. Many herbs are used differently from one culture to another, although some are used similarly all over the globe. And some well known in one area—China, for instance— are strangers elsewhere.

Discovering medicinal herbs can begin with the study of recent publications on the topic, progress to learning how to grow the herbs you would like to keep handy, and continue into preparing herbs for use in healing soaps. As your knowledge and experience grow, you may find yourself combining herbs in unique ways that suit you and your family best.

With this book, you can develop your hallmark brand of fine soap. Your soap can help heal wounds, smooth roughness, and bring calm. Your family and friends will love your soap, and perhaps they will share in your transformation, too.

2

LOVING YOUR SKIN

The Tiger has her beautiful fur coat, the Swan his feathered finery, the Dolphin a sleek water cloak, and the Bumble Bee a glistening flight jacket. Woodland boulders are draped with moss; trees are covered with bark.

Your own skin is no less a miracle than all of these, and thus deserves to be acknowledged, understood, loved, and nurtured. Skin is a living, breathing, conscious aspect of the body. It extends the care it receives to the entire being.

As the largest organ of the human body—with an average weight of twenty pounds—the skin is composed of millions of cells and performs many vital functions. It shields internal organs from ultraviolet light rays and from marauding bacteria and other foreign matter. The skin also helps eliminate waste matter and regulates temperature via perspiration.

Ultrasensitive to pleasure and pain, the skin serves as a sensory receptor in times of possible pleasure or danger. It also signals others by blushing with embarrassment and paling with fear. Your skin brightens when you are relaxed and happy. Conversely, it appears drawn and ashen when you feel sad. Massaging the skin and muscles produces mood-altering chemicals in the brain, enhancing the entire emotional and physical well-being of the fortunate receiver.

The skin is composed of three layers: the epidermis, the dermis, and the fatty layer. Each performs particular functions, and the health of each layer can be enhanced through special care-regimens. The outer layer of the skin is the epidermis, and it illustrates life's great circle. From the bottom of the epidermis, new skin cells form and rise; at the top, old cells slough off. The life cycle of these cells is twenty-eight to thirty days, though the cycle can be hastened by adverse conditions such as sun or windburn, abrasion, or lack of sleep.

The second layer of the skin, the dermis, contains

nerves, hair follicles, elastic connective tissues, blood vessels, and oil and sweat glands. The glands work in harmony to protect and lubricate the epidermis, and their secretions of oil, water, and salts maintain the skin's proper protective pH balance of 4.5 to 5.5.

The third layer of the skin, below the dermis, is the fatty layer, or subskin, composed of fat and muscle tissue. It protects the top skin—indeed, the entire body—from temperature changes and bacterial infections. The subskin serves as a protective cushion for the body, and its structural integrity is also responsible for the outer shape and form of the skin.

Conscious, Alive, and Well

Your skin displays as much liveliness as you do!

This is why healing and nurturing the skin should begin with self-awareness. Skin problems reflect the state of your health and well-being, as well as concern for your loved ones.

Loving and nurturing the skin starts with adequate nutrition, exercise, and rest. An excellent diet that includes plenty of fresh fruits, vegetables, and whole grains nourishes the skin. Adequate vitamins and minerals, particularly the B-complex vitamins, help keep skin healthy. Regular exercise, preferably in fresh air, encourages the optimal function of the inner layers of the skin. Sufficient rest is essential, for it nurtures the skin, as well as the body and mind. Each of these techniques of care helps relieve the stress and inner turmoil of everyday life that so often alters the color and texture of the skin.

Be kind to your skin by avoiding the sun's ultraviolet light rays that burn and toughen the skin. Any harsh weather—hot or cold—stresses the skin. Hot showers, facials, and saunas can shock and dry it. Air pollutants irritate the skin, and cosmetics can clog and choke it. Skin suffers in very humid or very dry climates if it does not receive special care.

Corrective skin care can be a self-reliant, intuitive, and creative process. Repairing aging or damaged skin, or maintaining healthy skin, includes proper cleansing, exfoliation, moisturizing, toning, and nourishing. With a small investment of daily loving kindness to your skin, enhanced appearance will be yours within less than a month. Love your skin, and it will return the gift by showing off your health and happiness.

3

FLOWER POWER: HEALING GIFTS FROM THE GARDEN

Dissatisfaction with Western medicine, coupled with a herbal renaissance in America, is reawakening healing instincts that have lain dormant for so long. . . . A magical, intangible process, healing is an art, not a science.

—Rosemary Gladstar, Herbalist and author

Learning how and why to incorporate Nature's healing plants into soap is an intuitive and creative pastime, in itself a healing experience that leads to serenity, strength, and greater health. The garden's timeless offerings of flowers, roots, fruits, and seeds nourish creativity, healing, and hope. We have a legacy of ancestral self-healing that helps us develop peace of mind and body today.

We nearly lost our ancient herbal-healing traditions through the tumult of recent history. Once honored and trusted, the use of herbs for self-healing became scorned as antiquated and superstitious. Health care, at one time the province of the individual, the family, and the community, became the domain of ever more specialized professionals. The common knowledge of healing, affordable and steeped with common sense, has become a controlled, costly, and often inaccessible commodity.

Now the pendulum has swung back, and people are once again seeking the knowledge and materials useful in healing.

FINDING HEALING HERBS

Gathering the herbs for your soothing skin-care creations can be done in the garden, in the wild, in the pharmacy or natural products store, or from your favorite mail-order source. Every herb included here contributes to health and wholeness when properly used; after using healing leaves, seeds, flowers, and roots in your soap, you may find yourself going on to read even more about these wonderful gifts from Mother Nature.

If you gather plants from the wild, your local herbalist or *Peterson's Guide to Medicinal Plants: Eastern and Central U.S.* by Steven Foster and James A. Duke will help you make positive identifications. Please be mindful of the following simple rules.

Your Herbal Garden: With the Moon in Mind

Lovingly tending your own herb garden extends the pleasure you will receive from your soapmaking and places you within the great annual cycle of the seasons. The quiet vibrancy of the garden nurtures those who give it time and energy. You can make a garden in the traditional way, by starting with a sunny patch of ground. Not possible? Try growing your herbs in containers that can be moved from place to place to take advantage of the best light. Even a bright windowsill affords some herbs a happy environment. But if your own garden is out of the question, visit the local farmers' market. There you may well find organic herbs that have been grown and harvested with the love and care that you would give them yourself.

- *Generally, gathering on public lands is allowed only if you have a permit. Each level of government in each location has differing policies on gathering plants, so protect the lands that belong to everyone by finding and following the rules that apply.*

- *On privately owned lands, seek permission of the owner before gathering.*

- *Educate yourself about what parts of the plant are useful, the best harvest time, and how you should prepare the plant for use in your soap.*

- *Positively identify the plant; if in doubt, don't harvest.*

- *Never harvest endangered plants or those that are plentiful in other areas but rare in yours.*

- *Gather only from well-established plots, leaving the healthiest plants to reproduce.*

- *Honor and appreciate the plant before picking.*

- *For your personal safety, and for healthy plants that are less affected by roadside pollution or spraying, do your gathering far away from traffic.*

You will do well to keep the moon in mind when working with your herb garden. This quiet yet formidable planetary neighbor affects the behaviors of the ocean, atmosphere, animals, humans, and plants. Lunar calendars and planting almanacs offer particular advice for planting and harvesting herbs in optimal synchronicity with the phases of the moon. Tradition says you should plant annuals, those that must be replanted every year, after the full moon (by the dark of the moon). Plant biennials, perennials, and root plants after the new moon (by the light of the moon). While some scoff at this advice, many an experienced gardener will confirm that in the garden, the moon makes a difference.

Renewed interest in herbal medicine has encouraged many plant nurseries and garden centers to stock seeds and plants useful in healing; while such plants may not be categorized as "medicinal," many are identified as herbs. Not all, however: The soothing *calendula officinalis,* so helpful in healing irritated skin, is better known as "pot marigold" and sold as a flowering plant. Look closely among the plants for those you want to use in your soap. If you have no local source of herb plants or seeds, consult the Resource Directory in the back of this book.

The energy of the moon also flows through the herbal harvest. Herbs for drying are best harvested just before the new moon. In general, the healing energy in roots is more pronounced at the new moon, so they should be dug just before it arrives. Leaves, fruits, flowers, and twigs are best gathered between the new and the full moon. By harvest time, you will know your herbs well, and indeed, I believe, they will know you, too.

PREPARING HERBS FOR SOAPMAKING

Most of the fresh herbs you gather from garden, field, or herb shop must be prepared for use in making soap, although a few can be added directly to your base. Fresh Aloe Vera and Nettle Leaf Soap on page 65 and Jewelweed Soap on page 49 use fresh plant emulsions to provide the beneficial qualities of the plants directly in the soap.

Drying Herbs. Perhaps the easiest way of preparing herbs is drying. Gather the herbs early in the morning, just after the dew has evaporated. Cutting at this time preserves the oils that give the plant its scent, flavor, and often its medicinal proper-

ties; in the heat of the day, these oils evaporate. Rinse the plants under cool water to remove dust.

To dry tall herbs, tie a handful of stems together with a string and hang upside down in a cool, shady, dry place such as a porch or garage. Place smaller herbs on paper towels in a shallow tray for drying. If necessary, use a small fan to circulate the air around the herbs. Turn or

stir them every other day. When the herbs are thoroughly dry, but before they become brown and brittle, place them in a tightly lidded jar and store them in a cool, dark place. Be sure to label your herbs, as many look alike after drying.

Herbs that dry well include sage, rosemary, lavender, and calendula. Your natural products store or herb shop will also have a selec-

30

tion of dried herbs suitable for use in soothing soaps.

Making Tinctures. Tinctures add intense healing power to soap. They are easy to make and have an excellent shelf life (some say years!). Tinctures are made by soaking fresh or dried herbs in a base of grain alcohol, vinegar, or glycerin. You may use fresh or dried plants. If you choose alcohol, be sure that it is safe to drink. Rubbing alcohol, for instance, is not; do not use it in your herbal preparations.

To make alcohol or vinegar-based tinctures, fill a clean pint jar with fresh herbs and cover with 190-proof grain alcohol, 100-proof vodka or brandy, or vinegar. Cap with a plastic lid or a new, undamaged canning-jar lid and shake for ten minutes. Shake once a day thereafter for four weeks. Store in a cool, dark place. Check the tincture after one week and add more alcohol or vinegar if needed to

Herbs are easily prepared as tinctures, infusions, decoctions, and oils.

keep the plants entirely submerged. After four weeks, strain and press the liquid through fine-weave cotton cloth. Discard the plants and store the tincture in dark glass. For dry herbs, pulverize half a cup and place in a clean pint jar. Pour two cups of alcohol or vinegar over them. Follow same storage and shaking procedures as for fresh-herb tinctures.

Making liquid-glycerin tinctures for soap is equally easy, and it makes perfect sense because glycerin enhances soap's overall feel and performance. Though liquid glycerin will not extract resins from herbs the way alcohol or vinegar does, it does extract other soothing elements such as the mucilage found in comfrey leaf and root. Liquid glycerin is available from the pharmacy.

If you're using dry herbs, place 1/2 cup of pulverized herbs in a clean pint jar. Mix together 1 1/2 cups glycerin and

31

1/2 cup sterilized water and add to the jar. Shake and store as described above.

Decoctions, Infusions, and Oils. Decoctions are strong teas made by simmering in water the hard, woody parts of herbs, such as roots, barks, grains, seeds, and nuts. The process captures the desired qualities of certain plants and imparts them to your soap. Begin your decoction by placing about 1/2 cup of plant material in a quart of water. Soak the herbs for several hours, then simmer for half an hour. Strain and store the liquid in the refrigerator until ready to use. Witch Hazel Soap—you'll find it on page 53—is a good example of a soap made with a decoction.

Infusions are delicate teas made by pouring hot, steamy water over fresh or dried plant parts. Three tablespoons of dried or fresh herb per cup of water, steeped ten minutes, will suffice; nonchlorinated water is best. Lavender and Rosemary Soap for blemished skin on page 56 is made with herbal infusions.

Herbal oils are prepared by soaking the fresh or dried herb in oil (I prefer organic olive oil for its stable nature) for a period of two weeks. The enhanced oil that results can be added to glycerin soap to attain special soothing qualities; add about one tablespoon of oil per cup of soap base.

Essential oils are made by either a distillation or mechanical extraction process. The equipment and knowledge of chemistry required to produce essential oils lies beyond the budget and learning of most folks, including myself. High-quality essential oils with wonderful natural properties can be purchased for soapmaking.

The recipes in this book were developed to make good use of herbs prepared in these ways. Whether you grow, gather, or purchase your herbs, these preparation methods allow you to enjoy their herbal goodness throughout the year.

4

NATURALLY HEALING SOAPS

Herbal soaps can become a soothing, effective part of your family's health-care regimen. With the following recipes, you'll make soap useful in fighting illness and infection and soap that helps clean wounds and eases the itch of poison ivy and insect bites. To bring out your skin's natural beauty, you'll make soaps and scrubs that are corrective, nourishing, and softening. The gentle glycerin soap base and healing herbs in these soaps will set you on the path to feeling better.

To complete the following recipes, you need a one-quart double boiler, measuring spoons and cup, stirring spoons or sticks (I like old chopsticks best), cheesecloth, and plastic soap or candy molds or plastic food-storage containers with an approximate capacity of two cups.

Each recipe requires that you melt the glycerin soap base in a double boiler over medium heat. Each recipe assumes that the glycerin soap base has already been melted into a liquid form.

Aside from the potential dangers of working around a stove and hot liquids, the entire process described herein is quite safe and can be recommended as a supervised project for children.

ANTISEPTIC SOAPS

Antiseptic herbal soaps can be helpful against bacteria, viruses, and fungi, the agents that most commonly infect the skin's surface. Used for washing, the herbs and the soaps work together to destroy and wash away infectious materials, thus supporting the skin's efforts to heal. In addition, washing household surfaces with antiseptic soaps helps maintain health by reducing the likelihood of infection. When there is illness in the household, using antiseptic soaps becomes important in preventing the spread of illness. Most importantly, despite all our modern germ-fighting strategies, the single most important thing we can do to maintain health is to wash our hands thoroughly and frequently, and I recommend these antiseptic soaps.

Common Plantain Soap
(Plantago major)

Plantain is a familiar and prolific broad-leafed wild weed. You have probably pulled it from your yard or garden, for plantain has become naturalized throughout the world.

Freshly gathered and macerated (mashed), plantain yields juice second to none as a wound healer, in part because of its mild antiseptic qualities. It helps stanch blood flow and reduces inflammation, too.

After washing a wound with Plantain Soap, make a poultice of fresh, mashed leaves warmed by adding enough boiling water to make a paste. Apply the poultice to the wound and hold it in place with a bandage. You will be pleased with how quickly your wound heals!

To include plantain's goodness in soap, blend a handful of the leaves with 1/4 cup glycerin and 1/8 cup water. Strain through cheesecloth and add according to directions below. If you are purchasing plantain in dried form, first make a plant oil as described on page 31; you may also purchase plantain oil ready-made.

Ingredients

2 cups glycerin soap base

1/4 cup strained plant juice/glycerin mixture

or

2 tablespoons plantain oil

Combine melted base and herbal materials. Stir until blended, then pour into molds and cool.

Goldenseal Soap
(Hydrastis canadensis)

Goldenseal is a versatile healer that attacks the bacteria, viruses, and fungi that cause contagious illness. Though sometimes found in the wild, it is rare, so it's best to grow it yourself or purchase it in powdered form. This herb's chief active constituents include the alkaloids berberine, hydrastine, and canadine.

For use in soap, goldenseal's rhizomes and roots are dried and pulverized. Goldenseal Soap works well as a wound-washing and sickroom soap.

Ingredients
2 cups glycerin soap base
3 teaspoons goldenseal powder mixed with 2 tablespoons olive oil
1 tablespoon goldenseal tincture

Add the herbal ingredients to the melted soap base. Mix until smooth and pour into molds. Cool and release. Keep the soap wrapped in opaque paper or in a dark place until ready for use.

Cloud's Healing Soap
(Calendula officinalis; Chamaecyparis thyoides; Symphytum officinale; Hydrastis canadensis)

Several years ago my dog, Cloud, was hit by a truck. By the time we found her, one foot was hanging by a shred of skin, and by the time we got her to the veterinarian, it was completely detached. Although the veterinarian cleaned her injury, reattached the foot, and put Cloud on a strong course of antibiotics, he warned that she was a prime candidate for gangrene. The prognosis was not good.

Cloud and I decided to put up a fight to save her foot. I used fresh comfrey poultices, cedar oil, goldenseal, and calendula; Cloud used patience, rest, and her own saliva to heal the wound. Over the next six months, Cloud healed. By the end of the year she had regained full use of her foot. So you can understand why I have so much faith in this combination of healing herbs.

Calendula flowers (pot marigold) are essential to this soap, and they are easy to grow in most gardens. Active against inflammation, swelling, and infection, calendula also offers an intoxicating scent and a healing feeling!

Comfrey leaf, with its high allantoin content, hastens healing by stimulating the growth of skin cells. Both cedar oil and goldenseal powder work against infection.

Ingredients

2 cups glycerin soap base
2 tablespoons calendula oil
1 teaspoon white cedar oil
3 tablespoons comfrey leaf powder
1 teaspoon goldenseal powder
1 tablespoon dried and pulverized calendula flowers (optional)

Mix well, pour into molds, and cool. Store in a dark place and use as a wash whenever infection threatens.

White Cedar Soap
(Chamaecyparis thyoides)

White cedar oil first caught my attention when an old-timer showed me a deep scar on his gnarly thumb. He had nearly severed the thumb while cutting cedar in 1936, he said, and subsequently the thumb became gangrenous.

Wisely, this man of the Great North Woods soaked his hand in white cedar oil for an hour a day. Within a week his condition had reversed, and it was not long before he recovered full health and use of the thumb.

I have since used white cedar soap for many of my wound-washing needs. I also favor it for washing hands and surfaces when there is illness in my family. The scent itself is clean and healing.

Ingredients

2 cups glycerin soap base

2 tablespoons decoction of fresh white cedar leaf (optional)

1 tablespoon white cedar essential oil

Combine melted base and herbal materials. Stir until blended, then pour into molds and cool.

Tea Tree Antiseptic Soap
(Melaleuca linariifolia)

Tea tree oil is an essential oil extracted by steam distillation from the leaves of a tree native to Australia. This ingredient is especially welcome in treating skin maladies because it is gentle and penetrates easily while working against bacteria, fungi, yeasts, and viruses. The soap is helpful in treating athlete's foot and wounds and preventing illness. It is also a fine deodorant soap.

Ingredients
2 cups glycerin soap base
2 tablespoons tea tree oil

Combine melted base and herbal oil. Stir until blended, then pour into molds and cool.

Poison Ivy Soaps

It seems that every part of North America has its own species of poison ivy. In the East there are *Rhus radicans* and *Rhus vernix;* in the West one finds *Rhus diversiloba,* known as poison oak. The plants contain the oil urushiol, which causes contact dermatitis in many. The skin may swell and itch, and rash with weeping blisters can follow. Especially severe reactions to *Rhus*-family plants include fever, headache, and malaise. The best ways to prevent reactions to poison ivy and its kin are to recognize and avoid the plants. If you suddenly notice you're standing in the middle of a patch of it, however, you can prevent a serious bout of itching and pain.

These anti-itching soaps should be used as soon after exposure to poison ivy as possible. Also wash clothing, shoes, and equipment that may carry the oil in strong soap and hot water. With prompt attention, you may well avoid the misery of poison ivy dermatitis.

Calamine Soap

Calamine lotion, long associated with easing the discomfort of poison ivy, originates not in the Plant Kingdom, but in the Mineral Kingdom. Calamine Soap's main ingredient is calamine, a pink powder consisting of zinc oxide mixed with a small amount of ferric oxide. In some areas you can purchase this wonder ingredient at your local pharmacy, but nearly everywhere you can obtain it in a familiar liquid form—calamine lotion. Calamine Soap is mild and soothing for any type of skin irritation, particularly those that cause itching.

Ingredients

1 tablespoon calamine powder (or 2 tablespoons calamine lotion)

1 tablespoon bentonite or cosmetic-grade clay

2 tablespoons liquid glycerin

1 cup glycerin soap base

Mix together the calamine, clay, and liquid glycerin until smooth, adding a small amount of water if needed. Whisk the mixture into the soap base, pour into molds, and cool. This soap will remain effective for two years.

Jewelweed Soap
(Impatiens pallida, Impatiens capensis)

Jewelweed grows anywhere that damp woods exist. It unfurls its butter-yellow flowers by mid-June and blooms until frost; flowers are followed by brittle seedpods that snap open at a touch. Mostly, however, this plant is called jewelweed because it "grows like a weed," and the backs of its leaves shimmer like silvery jewels when the plant is submerged in water (very magical).

By Mother Nature's generous plan, jewelweed thrives in soil and moisture conditions also favored by the plant for which it is a traditional antidote: poison ivy and its kin. So if you suddenly find yourself ankle-deep in poison ivy, your chances are good of finding jewelweed nearby. Crush jewelweed plants in your hands and rub the juices on your skin to prevent skin reactions.

For soap, jewelweed must be used in either fresh or frozen form. Once you locate a patch, snip about twenty plants at the base. Get them home as soon as you can. Rinse them in cool water and blend them with 1 cup of water and 1/2 cup of glycerin. Strain this maceration through several layers of cheesecloth, discarding the remaining plant matter.

You will need 1/2 cup of this mixture for the following soap recipe. Any remainder can be frozen into ice cubes and stored for direct application on future outbreaks of poison ivy.

Ingredients

2 cups glycerin soap base, cooled to a temperature of
135 to 140 degrees F
1/2 cup jewelweed maceration

Combine melted base and herbal materials. Stir until blended, then pour into molds and cool. Keep this soap wrapped in paper, or store it in a cool, dark place. It remains potent for one year.

Camphor and Clary Sage Soap
(Cinnamomum Camphora; Salvia Sclarea)

This soap has a real zing to it, as most camphorated products do. It is quite helpful in arresting the itch caused by insect bites and poison ivy outbreaks.

Camphor is a white crystalline substance distilled from the leaves, twigs, and branches of the *Cinnamonum Camphora* tree. Pungent and slightly cold to the touch, camphor oil numbs the peripheral sensory nerves and is mildly antiseptic.

Clary sage oil treats skin irritation by acting as a drying agent and reducing swelling. It is easy to grow in most gardens; if this herb is available to you fresh or dried, begin this recipe by making an infusion as discussed on page 31.

Ingredients

2 cups glycerin soap base

2 tablespoons camphor oil

1/4 cup clary sage infusion

and/or

1 teaspoon clary sage oil (optional)

Combine melted base and herbal materials. Stir until blended, then pour into molds and cool. Keep this soap wrapped or store in a cool, dark place. It will remain fully effective for eighteen months.

Balsam of Peru and Benzoin Anti-Itch Soap
(Myroxylon Balsamum; Styrax officinalis)

Balsam of Peru is a warmly aromatic resin useful against parasites such as scabies. It is also an excellent remedy for other types of skin irritation, including eczema and dermatitis caused by poison ivy or poison oak.

Benzoin is a balsamic resin that soothes irritated skin. Both ingredients are somewhat difficult to obtain in fresh form, but they are readily available in prepared tinctures.

Ingredients
2 cups glycerin soap base
1 tablespoon tincture of balsam of Peru
1 tablespoon tincture of benzoin

Combine melted base and herbal materials. Stir until blended, then pour into molds and cool. Store this soap wrapped in opaque paper.

Witch Hazel Soap
(Hamamelis virginiana)

Dried witch hazel bark is available through several mail-order herb suppliers. It can often be found in the herb department of natural products stores. As officially stated in the *United States Pharmacopoeia,* witch hazel bark contains the active constituents tannin and gallic acid. Preparations of the bark work against pain, slow bleeding, and are astringent and anti-inflammatory. Each of these qualities contributes to this soap's excellent ability to relieve the effects of poison ivy and other skin irritations.

Begin this recipe by making a decoction of the witch hazel bark as detailed on page 31. You will need about 1/4 cup of witch hazel bark and 2 cups of water. Strain and store the liquid in the refrigerator until ready to use.

Ingredients
2 cups glycerin soap base
1/4 cup witch hazel bark decoction

Combine melted base and herbal materials.
Stir until blended, then pour into molds and cool.
Store this soap in a dark, cool place.

SOAPS FOR BLEMISHED SKIN

Blemished skin is marked by chronic pustules, blackheads, whiteheads, and frequent scarring. Blemishes can be a problem at any age, but during the teenage years they often flare up because increased hormone production stimulates the skin's oil glands. When the excess oil and a buildup of dead skin cells clog the pores, bacteria thrive in the pores and pressure builds. Swelling, soreness, and infections damage the skin.

A thoughtful regimen of appropriate skin care, healthful diet, and exercise can make a world of difference. If your skin problems are persistent, consult a dermatologist. You also may wish to consult a doctor of chiropractic for relief, because some internal functions that improve the skin's health can be enhanced through spinal adjustments. The soaps in this section will gently support your return to trouble-free skin.

Lavender and Rosemary Soap
(Lavandula officinalis or angustifolia; Rosmarinus officinalis)

Lavender and rosemary have a mild yet stimulating effect on skin. Both are antiseptic, anti-inflammatory, and beneficial for treating wounds, blemishes, boils, dermatitis, herpes, fever blisters, and more! Begin this soap with an infusion of fresh lavender and rosemary, picked midmorning for highest oil content. Use some of each for a fresh infusion, proportioned as you like; dried herbs are effective, too. Steep the herbs together (see page 31 for infusions).

Ingredients

3 cups glycerin soap base

1/4 cup infusion of lavender flowers and rosemary leaves

1 1/2 teaspoon lavender oil

1/2 teaspoon rosemary oil

1 teaspoon pulverized dried rosemary (optional)

Combine melted base and herbal materials. Stir until blended, then pour into molds and cool. This soap is so pleasing—try not to give it all away! Store some in a linen closet for yourself and your family.

Chamomile, Sage, and Laminaria Seaweed Scrub Cleanser

(Anthemis nobilis; Salvia Sclarea; Laminaria digitata)

A mildly abrasive scrub cleanser exfoliates the surface of the skin, removing the dead and dying cells before they clog your pores. Used on a regular basis, the scrub can smooth scarring. Please note, however, that using a scrub on skin that is erupted will only aggravate, not help, the condition.

The following recipe calls for making a soap containing sage and seaweed and then shaving it into a mixture of dried chamomile flowers and powdered oatmeal. Chamomile and oatmeal are anti-inflammatory. Sage is an astringent and disinfectant.

Ingredients

1 cup glycerin soap base

1 tablespoon powdered laminaria seaweed

1 tablespoon clary sage oil

Combine melted base and herbal materials. Stir until blended, then pour into molds and cool. Shave with a cheese grater, finest shred. Add shavings to the following:

1 cup dried chamomile flowers, chopped

1/2 cup uncooked oatmeal; grind in a blender until coarse

Mix well and store in lidded, dark containers. To use, make a paste in the palm of your hand with 1 tablespoon of scrub cleanser and a little water. Gently rub on the face in a circular motion for one minute, then rinse.

Juniper Soap
(Juniperus)

A diverse genus, junipers are evergreens that are widely distributed and cultivated throughout the Northern Hemisphere. Hardy even in harsh climates and relatively trouble-free, juniper is favored in landscaping. Its small and fragrant blue berries are used in the production of gin and several types of medicinal and fragrant oils.

Juniper berries and juniper oil are antiseptic, astringent, and useful in the treatment of acne. Juniper berries can be collected during the summer and dried, macerated, and made into a tincture. The tincture and the essential oil can be used in the following recipe.

Ingredients

2 cups glycerin soap base

2 tablespoons tincture of juniper berries

1 teaspoon juniper essential oil

Combine melted base and herbal materials. Stir until blended, then pour into molds and cool.

Self-Heal Soap
(Prunella vulgaris)

Self-heal, also known as heal-all, is a common wild plant. With the help of your local herbalist or a good herb-identification book, chances are you'll find this beautiful little plant right in your backyard. Self-heal is astringent and slows bleeding. It is especially helpful for wounds and skin eruptions.

Collect the entire plant in early to mid-summer, after its purple flowers have appeared. Select twelve plants and at midmorning snip them at the base. At home, rinse the plants in cool water and put them in a blender with 1/4 cup of liquid glycerin and 2 tablespoons of water. Macerate and strain through several layers of cheese cloth.

Ingredients
2 cups glycerin soap base

plant/glycerin mixture prepared above

1 teaspoon of lavender oil (optional)

Mix well, pour into molds, and cool. Store in paper wrappers or in a cool, dark place. This soap remains effective for one year.

Ylang-Ylang and Frankincense Soap
(Cananga odorata; Burseraceae Boswellia)

Since most frankincense is imported from Somalia, and ylang-ylang comes from the Comoro Islands, you won't have to grow, gather, or forage the ingredients for this soap. They are readily available via mail order or from your favorite herb shop. This soap is an excellent choice for troubled skin, and it lifts the spirits, too.

In aromatherapy, the fragrance of ylang-ylang soothes anger and frustration. It also serves as an antidepressant, an aphrodisiac, and a euphoric. Ylang-ylang oil has a balancing effect on the sebaceous glands, and it serves to soften and rejuvenate the skin.

Frankincense is a dried gum resin from the frankincense tree. The resin is composed of boswellic acid and alibanoresin. Frankincense powder offers a slightly astringent action and promotes healing.

Ingredients

2 cups glycerin soap base

1/8 cup powdered frankincense mixed with

1/8 cup liquid glycerin

1 teaspoon ylang-ylang essential oil

Mix well, pour into molds, and cool. This soap has a shelf life of eighteen months.

SOOTHING EMOLLIENT
HEALING SOAPS

Emollients are conditioners that soothe and soften the skin. Emollient soaps will leave your skin feeling soft, supple, and nourished. With the exception of Pine Tar Soap, these soaps are good to use at any age and are excellent for any type of skin.

The following recipes are made with various grains, roots, butters, and botanical powders. They begin at the baby's bottom with Slippery Elm Soap and work their way to the top of the head with Pine Tar Soap for eczema, psoriasis, and dandruff.

Baby's Bottom Repair Soap
(Ulmus fulva; Myroxylon Balsamum)

The inner bark of the slippery elm tree has long been recognized for its medicinal virtues. Its abundant mucilage imparts wonderfully soothing and healing qualities to soap. For use in soap making, purchase slippery elm in powdered form.

Balsam of Peru is extremely good for chapped skin. It is also a good antiseptic and blends well in soap. In addition, it has a sweet vanillin "baby scent" and a complementary measure of first aid. I highly recommend this soap for the prevention and treatment of diaper rash.

Ingredients

2 cups glycerin soap base

3 tablespoons slippery elm powder

1 tablespoon vegetable glycerin

1 tablespoon balsam of Peru oil

Mix together slippery elm, vegetable glycerin, and balsam of Peru oil until smooth. Add to glycerin soap base. Mix well and pour into molds. Cool and store, wrapped in opaque paper.

Fresh Aloe Vera and Nettle Leaf Soap
(Aloe vera; Urtica dioica)

Aloe vera is a very special healing plant—kind to sunburned skin, and enriching and soothing to normal, oily, or dry skin. Aloe gel is best taken directly from the leaves, even though the soft-hearted may feel squeamish about amputating a limb of a favorite house plant. You can buy prepared aloe juice if you want to.

I've had my faithful aloe vera plant for over seventeen years, and I always approach it with due love and respect. If it could speak in words, I believe it would say that it likes to help me, that it has plenty of leaves, and that it does not mind giving one up occasionally, as long as I make my slice quickly and with fair warning.

When I need fresh aloe vera, I select a juicy leaf and remove it quickly with a sharp knife. I lay it on a plate and make a lengthwise incision and use a spoon to scrape out the gel. A spatula is useful to slide the gel into a measuring cup.

The second ingredient in this soap is nettle leaf. I prefer the dried leaf, but if you gather this herb fresh, protect your hands with impermeable leather or rubber gloves and transport the herbs in disposable paper bags.

The nettle's "sting" is caused by a fine fuzz that carries formic acid, creating pain when it brushes against the skin. The acid dissipates, however, when the nettle leaf is simmered, so place the leaves briefly in hot water and macerate them. The nettle leaves, when dried, impart a pretty green fleck to the soap and provide a stimulating quality.

Ingredients

1 cup glycerin soap base

1/8 cup aloe vera gel

2 tablespoons crushed dried nettle leaf

or

2 tablespoons simmered, macerated fresh leaf

Mix together, pour into molds, and cool. Store in a dark cool place.

Oat and Barley Soap

No one can deny the gentle gifts offered by simple oatmeal and barley powder. The feel, the scent, and the soft beauty of their natural color make them welcome ingredients in soap.

Oats and barley are healing grains. They are rich in vitamins and minerals. They soothe sensitive skin, moisturize dry skin, and relieve itching, irritation, and inflammation. Beta glucan, an ingredient extracted from oat bran, is often used as a humectant to penetrate and deeply moisturize the skin. The following recipe uses both powdered grains and a slurry that is made from the cooked grains.

To begin this recipe, cook 1/4 cup of oatmeal and 1/4 cup of rolled barley in 1 1/2 cups of boiling water at medium heat for 15 minutes. Cool the mixture and place into a double layer of cheesecloth. Squeeze out and collect as much liquid slurry as you can; discard the remaining grain.

Ingredients

1 cup glycerin soap base

1/4 cup grain slurry

1/2 cup crushed or powdered oatmeal

1 teaspoon barley powder

Mix, pour into molds, and cool. This is a good all-over soap that nourishes both dry and oily skin without irritation.

Shea Butter Soap

Shea butter is the star ingredient in this soap. Also known as karite, this "butter" is a rich and creamy oil extracted from the fruit of an African tree valued for this product. Directly applied to the skin, shea butter will increase epidermal thickness and is said to hold certain sun-protection properties.

In this recipe, shea butter acts as a superfatting agent. Its qualities make a soap that is highly emollient and soothing for all types of skin. To scent this soap, add several drops of your favorite essential oil.

Ingredients

2 cups glycerin soap base

2 tablespoons shea butter, melted separately

Several drops of your favorite essential oil (optional)

Mix well, pour into molds, and cool.

Pine Tar Soap and Shampoo Bar

(Pinus sylvestris)

I feel confident in saying that this is the worst-smelling soap in the solar system! Despite its terrible scent, however, its virtues are unsurpassed as an effective home remedy for eczema, psoriasis, and dandruff. Pine tar is the culprit here! It is an impure turpentine, viscid and brown-black in color, produced by the distillation of roots of various conifer trees. It smells *horrible.* I highly recommend making this soap outside or in a well-ventilated area.

Pine tar acts as a cutaneous stimulant and antiseptic. To use this soap as a shampoo, simply rub the bar on wet hair until a lather is produced. Leave the shampoo on the scalp for several minutes before rinsing.

Ingredients

1 cup glycerin soap base
1 tablespoon castor oil (or olive oil)
1 tablespoon pine tar

Mix well, pour into molds, and cool. Keeps well for many years in a closed container.

5

THE ESOTERICS

The esoterics are a genre of soaps reflective of our times. I believe that they will be made by a new generation of soap makers for soap lovers with fresh thoughts on their minds. An esoteric soap has a mysterious, unseen quality to it, an aura of energy that changes in accordance with the physiological, emotional, and biofeedback fluctuations of the user. More importantly, the esoteric nature of the soap helps users to consciously shift personal rhythms (or frames of mind) from one state of being to another.

For example, the soap may help the user shift from feeling disconnected and separated from nature to feeling reconnected and nourished or energized by nature (see the recipe for Lightning Water Soap); from feeling overwhelmed and harried to feeling quiet and peaceful within (compliments of Moonbeam Soap); from feeling sad or depressed to feeling hopeful and capable (try a flower-essence soap). Do you have an "impossible" deadline to meet that will require you to become a super nova? Try Sunflower Soap! The esoterics will help people realize the power of their own thoughts to bring forth their own (and, thereby, others') joy, peace, and states of shared happiness.

FLOWER ESSENCE SOAP

Do you find yourself easily discouraged by minor setbacks? Do you cry, become fearful, or give up easily? Use gentian.

Are you tense, impatient, or easily irritated? You don't have to be! Use impatiens.

Feeling overwhelmed by duties and responsibilities? Elm will help you learn how to say NO!

Dr. Edward Bach (1886-1936), an English bacteriologist and homeopathic physician, spent years in conscious communion with the life force of hundreds of different flowers. His scientific work led him to believe that strong emotions and human conflict were the underlying causes of pain and illness, and that Mother Nature would reveal the secrets to healing these difficulties from within. Noticing that he felt particular influences when he held his hand over a flower,

This system of treatment is the most perfect that has been given to mankind within living memory. . . . they who will obtain the greatest benefit . . . . will be those who keep it as pure as it is; free from science, free from theories, for everything in Nature is simple.

—*Dr. Edward Bach*

he began to study these natural "vibrations".

From this work, Bach discovered a method for capturing the healing vibrations or the "Flower Essences". Thirty-eight different flowers, he believed, are willing to assist humans in healing emotional difficulties by awakening healthy natural rhythms and vibrations and transforming negative or limiting emotions and attitudes into more healthful and holistic ways of being. He identified seven types of remedies: For Fear, For Uncertainty, For Apathy, For Loneliness, For Over-sensitivity to Influences and Ideas, For Despondency or Despair, For Over-Care for the Welfare of Others.

Flower essences are a delight to make. First, research or intuit which flower variety you wish to use. While many people employ Bach's remedies, you may find that you and your own flowers will have unique experiences.

For instance, Bach recommends wild roses for those who seek to overcome a tendency to drift through life without goals or willfulness. Others, however, have reported that the essence of wild roses fills them with a playful joy.

To select flowers from your garden, hold your hand over a bloom and quietly meditate. Try this with several types of flowers; one will seem more willing than others to help you.

Flower Essence Soap

To make flower essence, you will need a quiet frame of mind, a sunny morning filled with fresh flower blossoms, a clean one-quart glass bowl, and scissors or clippers. Fill the bowl three-quarters full with sterilized, room-temperature springwater.

Approach the flowers in an appreciative, intentional, and thoughtful manner. Holding the bowl in one hand, snip the flowers into the water without touching them. Set the bowl of flowers on the ground in partial sun near the flower patch and leave undisturbed for several hours; then carefully remove the flowers from the bowl with a stem, and strew about the patch.

Preserve the flower essence by adding one cup of organic cider vinegar to the liquid, and bottle the essence in dark glass.

Ingredients
1 cup glycerin soap base
20 drops flower essence

Mix and pour into molds. Cool. Label each bar with the purpose of the soap and use accordingly.

SUNSHINE, MOONBEAM, AND LIGHTNING TEAS

Sunshine, moonbeam, and lightning teas are fun to make and magical to use as both a healing beverage and soap ingredient. For sunshine or moonbeam tea, simply place your favorite fresh or dried herbs in a clean, clear glass jar and fill with sterilized spring water. Cover and set in full sunlight or moonlight for several hours before straining.

For lightning water, set out empty, flat pans (glass or plastic) during the next thunderstorm.* The water collected in the pans will carry a special lightning charge and can be used in a variety of creative ways. In need of a boost? Imagine your next shower with a bar of Lightning Water Soap!

*If you live in an area troubled by air pollution, do not make lightning water.

Moonbeam Soap

The moon and the herb mugwort (*Artemisia vulgaris*) are the shining stars of this soap recipe. Mugwort, when hung near the bed or sewn into a pillow, will stimulate dreaming. If you would like a dreamy soap that encourages introspection, make a moonbeam tea of the mugwort several days after the full moon, when the moon is waning.

If you would like a soap that is more stimulating and activating, make moonbeam tea the day *before* or *on* the eve of the full moon. The power of the moon enhances the strength of the plant.

Any mugwort moonbeam tea not used in the soap can be added to your next bath. For a complete experience, bathe with Moonbeam Soap, sleep with a "dream pillow" made with dried mugwort leaves, and keep a journal near your bed to record your wonderful dreams.

Ingredients

2 cups glycerin soap base

1/2 cup mugwort moonbeam tea

1 tablespoon crushed and dried mugwort leaves

Mix well and pour into molds. Cool and release the soap. Store for use when dreams and introspection are desired.

Lightning Water Soap

Happenstance and thirst in the Great North Woods led me to my first drink of lightning water, fifteen years ago. At the time, my primary occupation was to lead people on wilderness excursions in the Adirondack Mountain Wilderness. On the first day of a twenty-day trip, I realized none of my ten clients had experience away from the comforts of modern life. In the driving August rain, their doubts and fears were evident.

Thunderstorm after thunderstorm moved through, exposing my slickered charges to blasts of rain, but we slogged two miles to our campground. First we set up our 6' by 8' nylon rainfly between the trees and huddled there, strangers together, some terrified of death by lightning. As the fearless leader of the moment, my job was to . . . be funny. The rain fly had caught at least a gallon of "lightning water", so I asked, over the drone of the relentless rain, "Is anyone thirsty?"

As everyone burst into laughter, I did a sales pitch for lightning water, "a traditional Northwoods cure for the fainthearted," I said. "Here, try some!"

We shared the water, and all felt rejuvenated immediately. Lightning Water Soap will keep you tuned into the unpredictable and strike you as something totally different and thrilling!

Ingredients

2 cups glycerin soap base

1/2 cup lightning water

Several drops of your favorite essential oil for scent (optional)

Mix well and pour into molds. Cool and store.
Use for an uplifting and rejuvenating bath or shower.

Sunflower Soap *(Helianthus annuus)*

Priestesses in the Incan temples of the Sun were crowned with sunflowers and cradled the flowers like sunbeams in their arms. Great reverence was bestowed on the sunflower, as it is now, for it offers bloom, seed, and oil.

Each of these gifts can be incorporated into Sunflower Soap. The petals of the bloom are made into a sunshine tea, providing golden radiance and warmth. The oil is added as an emollient, and the seeds are ground into a meal for the exfoliation and nourishment of the skin. Use the soap to begin your day with a shower of sunshine and the sunflower's three gifts.

Start this recipe by making Sunflower Tea: Place one cup of sunflower petals into a clean, clear jar. Cover the petals with one cup of cool water. Place the jar in a sunny place for several hours. Strain the liquid; discard petals.

Ingredients

2 cups glycerin soap base

4 tablespoons Sunflower Tea

2 tablespoons sunflower oil

2 tablespoons raw, hulled, and unsalted sunflower seeds, pulverized

1 teaspoon heliocarrot oil for golden color (optional)

Melt the glycerin soap base in a double boiler over simmering water.

Stir in other ingredients.

Pour liquid into flexible molds and cool.

6

THE HAVEN OF WATER

Welcome to the delight of the bath. Before stepping in, imagine the erasure of all the faces of all the clocks in the world. All radios, televisions, computers, and digital counters have stopped. All alarms are dismantled, all watches locked away, all cuckoos asleep, all pendulums still, all bell towers silent, all hourglasses emptied of sand.

In the name of our own sanity and well-being, we must transform the stressful, burdensome pace of life, including our perception of time. Most of us see time as an enemy, a fast-moving thief of relaxation and rejuvenation. Hurrying to catch up is fruitless; it is in the slowing, the stopping to rest and savor, that we stop the theft of our time and energy. Then we begin to enjoy the ordinary moments in life, the source of our deepest peacefulness and profound satisfactions. Through awareness, free will, and purpose, we can set aside the societally imposed pressures to hurry and let only the progression of the celestial bodies overhead and the individual beating of the heart become our measure.

THE PURPOSEFUL BATH

Special baths have been employed in every human culture to shift the frame of mind and rhythm of the psyche. In the ritual bath, time stops. Ease, relaxation, and peace replace tension and stress. During these interludes, creative inspirations and answers to life's deepest questions are brought into the realm of consciousness. From this bath, one can arise with new ideas, new insights, or simply a new appreciation for the value of a calm, quiet, and soothing bath.

Ritual baths have been a part of human culture for centuries. In 425 B.C., Herodotus wrote of the bathing customs of the Scythians, who placed certain fruits on the fire and inhaled the fumes. According to Homer, hot-air baths were called *laconia*. The Romans enjoyed the *balneum*, small bath chambers using heated waters. Steam bathing was embraced by the prophet Muhammed around A.D. 600.

The Finnish sauna, the Swedish bath, and the African steam hut of Liberia are all ancient forms of special baths. The Japanese enjoy several types. The Native American sweat lodge ceremony is a cleansing and purification ritual that seeks to heal body and spirit. All over the world, hot springs have been revered as places of healing and power.

Stepping In. The energy forces of water are unique, for water forms the basis of all life. Water captures and holds the vibrational characteristics of other substances. The sound and feel of falling, bubbling, or rushing water has long been recognized for its healing qualities. Warm water has a sedative and relaxing effect, while cool water refreshes and stimulates; the safest bath temperatures range from 75 degrees F to 105 degrees F. For bathing, nonchlorinated water is desirable, and some enjoy the soft, healing effects of sulfur water.

Creating a ritual bath for yourself in your own home or back yard provides a timeless freedom. You may play the Merlin of the magic waters, Goddess Pelé of the fiery volcanoes, or the child of the flowers—in the ritual bath, everyday concerns are shed.

DESIGNING YOUR OWN BATH

Do you need to relax and restore, or inspire and energize? Have you been overwhelmed with too much noise and pollution? Do you feel a cold coming on? A special bath can be tailored to your needs with help from herbal soaps, oils, and infusions.

Setting the Mood. The setting of your exquisite bath is limited only by your imagination. It could be the tub in your bathroom, a hot tub in a hotel, an outdoor hot tub, or a natural hot spring. A beautiful moonlit pond on a hot August night or a nook in a cool, rushing stream on a hot sunny day would also suffice rather nicely.

Wherever you choose to be, do everything possible to make your bath a pleasure for all the senses. Beauty to please the gaze could include an atrium of lush potted plants and fresh flowers, alive with scents and colors, or your favorite objects. Add scents that provoke warm memories, and textures ranging from the smooth, slick soap to a bristly bath brush to enhance the bath. A cooling drink, or a hot one if you prefer, adds sensual dimension.

Finally, surround yourself in quietude and privacy bro-

ken only by the sounds of nature, live or recorded. Turn the telephone ringers off, secure the doors, and in every way protect against intrusions and interruptions.

Candles give the bath area a quiet, golden glow and cast fascinating shadows, especially in a steamy room. The soft light of fire will ease your mind and calm your senses. Initiate the bath with many different candles burning and then extinguish them, one by one, as you journey deeper into serenity and savored relaxation.

Herbal Baths. Enjoy the therapeutic benefits of herbs while relaxing in your warm and nurturing bath. When medicinal and fragrant herbs and flowers are added to a bath, the essences travel into the body via the breath and pores of the skin. They affect the biochemistry and gently alter moods, stimulate healing, and alleviate symptoms of illness. There are many wonderful books available on the topic of aromatherapy and healing with herbs. Some are mentioned in the bibliography.

Are you troubled by headaches? I've found that they're eased by the herbs eucalyptus, peppermint, lemongrass, lavender, or chamomile.

If premenstrual syndrome is a problem, soak with juniper, clary sage, cypress, fennel, tarragon, or rose. These herbs ease tension and lift the spirits.

If a cold has brought you low, try eucalyptus, lime, pine, tea tree, camphor or laurel scents to clear your airways and bring relief. Steam alone helps a cold, but when combined with helpful herbs it unleashes powerful curative powers.

Waning passion can be enlivened by a bath containing ginger, neroli, jasmine, patchouli, rose, or geranium. These herbs are both relaxing and invigorating; they help the troubles of the world drop away.

The benefits of these herbs are yours when you place drops of the essential oils into the warm bath and the scent rises. You may also toss small cloth bags of dried, blended herbs into the tub to add soft, gentle scents to the water. For a divine experience, float fresh, highly scented flowers on the water's surface!

THE BATH AS A GIFT

Have you ever watched the pure joy with which children experience a tub, pond, pool, or lakeside beach? Whenever children approach the magic of water, the spirit of playfulness joins them promptly.

Alas, we adults seldom experience the freedom of this play, but this need not be so. Hot tubs, natural hot springs, and commercial spas have become very popular as places where adults can meet,

90

enhancing friendships, intimacy, and good feelings. The mood is of our own creation: laughing and splashing as we wash away the tension of the work week, or quietly relaxing as we review and set aside recent events. In laughter or shared silence, in conversation and mutual appreciation, the shared bath is one of life's simple joys. Enhance these baths with skin-smoothing soap such as Shea Butter Soap, candlelight, fragrant herbs, and special food and drink; chilled juices and fruits are especially welcome.

You can also make a special bath a remarkable gift to friend or loved one. Do you have a friend struggling with a life change or trying to overcome personal difficulty? You may be helpless to solve the problems, but you can soothe your friend's spirit with a specially prepared bath.

Prepare the bath with care for all the senses, as you be-

lieve your friend will prefer, and make special soaps available. If tension is a problem, select White Cedar Soap or Juniper Soap for their calming scents, and strengthen these herbs by adding essential oils such as clary sage and clove to the bath water. Perhaps your friend will enjoy the skin-softening effects of Baby's Bottom Repair Soap and its light vanillin scent, or the emollient properties of Shea Butter Soap. While your friend enjoys the bath, prepare a warm robe and towels, a soothing drink, and a light meal.

This gift from one heart to another can be transformed to a romantic bath for or with one's beloved. Like a courting ritual, a special bath on a special occasion, such as a wedding night or anniversary, can make the occasion even more memorable.

The pleasures of the bath can be for any season or any reason in life. They are yours to create and enjoy. For yourself or another, the bath is a gift of timelessness and creative healing.

Bibliography/ Recommended Reading

Bach, Edward. *The Bach Flower Remedies.* New Cannan, CT: Keats Publishing, 1931.

Bruchac, Joseph. *The Native American Sweatlodge History and Legends.* Freedom, CA: Crossing Press, 1993.

Callan, Annette. *Skin Wise: A Guide to Healthy Skin for Women.* Aukland, NY: Oxford Press, 1990.

Cameron, Myra. *Mother Nature's Guide to Vibrant Beauty and Health.* Englewood Cliffs, NJ: Prentice-Hall, 1990.

Cavitch, Susan M. *A Soapmaker's Companion, A Comprehensive Guide with Recipes, Techniques, and Know-How.* Pownal, VT: Storey Publications, 1997.

de Haas, Cheri. *Natural Skin Care.* New York: Avery Publishing Group, 1987.

Failor, Catherine. *Transparent Soapmaking.* Portland: Rose City Press, 1997.

Fischer-Rizzi, Susanne. *Complete Aroma Therapy Handbook.* New York: Sterling Publishing, 1990

Foster, Steven, and James A. Duke. *Peterson Field Guide to Medicinal Plants—East Central Region.* New York: Houghton Mifflin, 1990.

Gladstar, Rosemary. *Herbal Healing for Women.* New York: Simon and Shuster, 1993.

Grieve, Maude. *A Modern Herbal.* New York: Dover Publications, 1931.

Gurudas. *Flower Essences and Vibrational Healing.* San Rafael, CA: Cassandra Press, 1989.

Gurudas. *The Spiritual Properties of Herbs.* San Rafael, CA: Cassandra Press, 1988.

Hanh, Thich Nhat. *Peace Is Every Step.* New York: Bantam Books, 1991.

Krueger, Treila. *All Clear.* New York: Betterway Publications, Inc., 1984.

Loughran, Joni. *Natural Skin Care: Alternative and Traditional Techniques.* Berkeley, CA: Frog, Ltd., 1996.

Minter, Sue. *The Healing Garden: A Natural Haven for Body Senses and Spirit.* London: Headline, 1993.

Rechtschaffen, Stephen. *Timeshifting: Creating More Time to Enjoy Your Life.* New York: Doubleday, 1996.

RETAIL MAIL-ORDER SOURCES

Each source has a code [i.e., (P)]. Use this code to determine which company carries the soapmaking products you want to obtain. Products are listed on page 95.

Avena Botanicals (A)
219 Mill Street
Rockport, Maine 04856
(207) 594-0694
High quality, organically grown herbs and herbal preparations. Catalog $2.00

Companion Plants (C)
7247 N. Coolville Ridge Rd.
Athens, Ohio 45701
(614) 592-4643
Herbal plants and seeds. Catalog: $3.

Ellon USA, Inc. (E)
644 Merrick Road
Lynbrook, NY 11563-2332

(800) 4 BE CALM
Flower essences and homeopathic products.

Frontier Herb Cooperative (F)
P.O. Box 299
Norway, IA 53218
(800) 669-3275
Wide selection of herbal products and oils. Catalog: Free.

Life of the Party (LP)
832 Ridgewood Ave., Bldg. #2
North Brunswick, NJ 08902
(908) 828-0886
Plastic soap molds.

Llewellyn Worldwide (L)
P.O. Box 64383
St. Paul. MN 55164-0383
(800) THE MOON
Lunar calendars and books.

Pegasus Products (P)

P.O. Box 228
Boulder, Colorado 80306-0228
(800) 527-6104
e-mail: starvibe@indra.com
web: www.pegasusproducts.com
FAX: (970) 667-3624
Flower essences and more.

Pourette (POUR)
P.O. Box 17056
Seattle, WA 98107
(206) 789-3188
Catalog: $6.00

SunFeather Natural Soap Company (SUN)
1551 Hwy. 72
Potsdam, NY 13676
(315) 265-3648
Kits, books, videos, software, equipment, and raw materials for soapmakers. Glycerin soap base, soapmakers club and newsletter. Home-party plan. Catalog: $3.

Aloe vera: F

Balsam of Peru: F

Bentonite or cosmetic-grade clay: F, SUN

Benzoin: F

Books on soapmaking: SUN, POUR

Calamine and calamine lotion: local pharmacy

Calendula: F

Camphor: F

Castor oil: SUN

Chamomile: F

Cheesecloth: Grocery store

Clary sage: F, SUN

Comfrey: F, SUN

Flower essences: F, E, A, P

Frankincense: F

Glycerin: F

Glycerin soap base: SUN, POUR

Glycerin soap-base recipe books: SUN

Goldenseal: F

Heliocarrot oil: SUN

Herb plants: C

Herb seeds: C

Juniper: F

Lavender: F, SUN

Laminaria seaweed: SUN

Lunar calendars: L

Mugwort: F

Nettle: F, A

Pine tar: Local pharmacy

Plantain leaves: F

Plantain oil: F

Rosemary: F, SUN

Self-heal: F

Shea butter: SUN

Slippery elm: F

Soap molds: LP, SUN

Soapmaking equipment: SUN, POUR

Sunflower petals: F

Sunflower oil F, grocery store

Sunflower seeds, raw and hulled: Grocery store or farm store

Tea tree oil: F, SUN

White cedar oil: F, SUN

Witch hazel: F

Ylang-ylang: F

Index

alcohol 30, 31
aloe vera 65
Anthemis nobilis 57
antiseptic soaps 39
aromatherapy 61
Artemisia vulgaris 80
Baby's Bottom Repair Soap 64
Bach, Dr. Edward 75–76
balsam of Peru 52
Balsam of Peru and Benzoin Anti-Itch Soap 51
barley 67
bath as gift 90–92
bath, herbal, 90
bath, ritual 88
bentonite clay 48
benzoin 52
Burseraceae Boswellia 61
calamine 48
Calamine Soap 48
calendula 29, 43
calendula officinalis 29, 43
camphor 51
Camphor and Clary Sage Soap 51
Cananga odorata 61
castor oil 69
Chamaecyparis thyoides 43, 44
chamomile 57
Cinnamomum Camphora 51
clary sage 51, 57
Cloud's Healing Soap
comfrey 43

Common Plantain Soap 40
cosmetic-grade clay 48
dandruff 69
decoctions 31
dermatitis 47, 56
dermis 21
drying herbs 30
Duke, James A. 27
eczema 69
emollients 63
epidermis
Esoterics 73
essential oils
Flower Essence Soap 77
flower essences 75–76
Foster, Steven 27
frankincense 61
Fresh Aloe Vera and Nettle Leaf Soap 65
gathering herbs 27–28, 49, 77
Gladstar, Rosemary 27
glycerin 15, 31
glycerin soap base 15
goldenseal 41, 43
Goldenseal Soap 41
hamamelis virginiana 53
herb 16
herb plants, seeds 29
herpes, 56
Hydrastis canadensis 41, 43
Impatiens capensis 49
Impatiens pallida 49
infusions 32
insect bites 51
jewelweed 49

Jewelweed Soap 49
Juniper Soap 59
Juniperus 59
karite 68
Laminaria digitata 57
laminaria seaweed 57
lavender 56, 60
Lavender and Rosemary Soap 56
Lavandula angustifolia 56
Lavandula officinalis 56
lightning water 79
Lightning Water Soap 81
maceration 40, 49, 65
Melaleuca linariifolia 45
moon lore 29
Moonbeam Soap 80
mugwort 80
Myroxylon Balsamum 51, 64
Oat and Barley Soap 67
oatmeal 57, 67
oils, essential 32
oils, herbal 31
parasites 52
pine tar 69
Pine Tar Soap and Shampoo Bar 69
Pinus sylvestris 69
plant identification 27
Plantago major 40
poison ivy 47, 49, 52, 56
pot marigold
poultice 40
Prunella vulgaris 60

psoriasis 69
Rhus family 47
rosemary 56
Rosmarinus officinalis 56
sage 51, 57
Salvia Sclarea 51, 57
Self-Heal Soap 60
Shea Butter Soap 68
skin 21–22
skin care 22, 55
skin health 22
skin, blemished 55, 60
slippery elm 64
stinging nettle 65
Styrax officinalis 51
subskin 22
Sunflower Soap 82
sunflower tea 82
Symphytum officinale 43
Tea Tree Antiseptic Soap 45
tinctures 30
Ulmus fulva 64
Urtica dioica 65
urushiol 47
vinegar 31, 77
white cedar oil 43, 44
White Cedar Soap, 44
witch hazel 53
Witch Hazel Soap 53
wound treatment 40, 41, 43, 56
ylang-ylang 61
Ylang-Ylang and Frankincense Soap 61